AF333737

BECOMING

all that God created me to be

Jennifer Wagenmaker

www.winesappress.com

Published 2012 by Winesap Press
Printed in USA
Cover and interior design by Eric Wagenmaker Design
Cover photo ©iStockphoto.com/javarman3
The text of this book is set in Minion Pro.
12 13 14 15 16   5 4 3 2 1
First Edition

Hardcover edition: 978-0-9859917-1-5
Paperback edition: 978-0-9859917-0-8
Ebook edition: 978-0-9859917-2-2

Dedication

The Lord has been more faithful than any friend to me.

My beloved husband—I am captivated by your love. I know the Lord brought you to me exactly when I needed you to join me in life. I anticipate our future together in Him with open arms. I know the best is yet to come.

My four sons—You are each so precious to me. Words cannot describe the depth of my love for you. Thank you for believing in me and pushing me to chase after my dreams. I promise to always do the same for you.

Mom & Dad—I consider myself one of the luckiest girls in the world to have been able to have such amazing and loving parents. Thank you both for your unconditional support in my life.

Dad & Cindy and Mom & Ron—Thank you so much for loving me the way you do. I am so blessed to have you.

To each of my brothers and sisters—I'm inspired by each one of you. I know we'll all finish strong and continue to push each other along on the way.

Ben—My editor. There is absolutely no way that I could have written this book without you! Thank you so much for your countless hours spent on this project and for helping me to reach my dream.

Tana—I am savoring this season with you, friend. Thank you for your love for our Savior. Dreaming with you about the things deep within our hearts.

Legacy Ladies—Anne, Christy, Corrine, Kristen, Melissa & Tana. To the ends of the earth (Isaiah 61).

My Girls—Dani (who helped me with this book), Erin, Jen, Alli, Kristen, Mary, Marcia, Amanda, Kendra, Carollee, Sophia, and Becky—I am so honored to have you as friends. Dream big, girls, and keep looking up.

To my pastor Justin and his wife Anne—Thank you both for your obedience and willingness to pick up your lives and to serve across the country for the kingdom. You have been easy to follow.

Table of Contents

Foreword

Jennifer Wagenmaker's love for Jesus Christ could easily be compared to taking a bucket of gasoline, spilling it out in a strategic manner to spell out the word "passion," and then lighting it on fire. She has the draw of a God-sized magnet, attracting people to the church and also to the cross.

I have had the pleasure of having Jen and Eric's presence on my team since our church began in a living room. One major reason why we were able to grow from a dream to being an actual church is God's grace shining on Jen and Eric and their being relentless followers and speakers of the gospel.

I was once walking into the hospital with Jen to visit a friend, and as we were walking in we saw a woman looking under her car for a cat. Jen invited her to church within fifteen seconds. Why? Because the woman had lost her cat and she was broken, needing a Savior? Either that, or Jen didn't need a reason! That is just who she is. "Hi my name is Jen, you need to know Jesus deeper." She is a constant invitation to know a real Jesus, in a real relationship, stripping off the religious tendencies and predictable masks.

Her story is raw, relatable, and readable. In the same way she invites everyone she meets into the gospel, her

book will challenge you to go deeper in your understanding of who God is. By doing so, she will invite you too!
May you accept the invitation.

Justin Thornton
Lead Pastor, Jericho Road Church

Introduction

We each have a story.

Story is a loaded word, both simple and also complex. It is beautiful, yet often hides a painful past. But all of humanity has this in common—we all have one. As simple and enchanting as that sounds, a great variable lies within each of us that holds the potential for great things. It is a crucial variable, that choice of whether or not we choose to share this story.

Though everyone has a story, they often look entirely different from one another. If you were to look back on your life, you would surely find some form of pain. Our past experiences shape us, and no matter how we choose to deal with them, they will continue to be part of our future.

I did not understand the healing that could take place in my heart until I was willing to share my story. But I had to choose to relive some of the pain and also begin to deal with it. I have been inspired to embrace my past, which will, in turn, help shape my future.

My prayer is that as you read this book you will be inspired to take comfort in your own past pain, knowing that it will help you to discover its purpose in your story as well as the role it plays in your future. It is my hope that you will recognize how close your Creator is to you as you embrace your journey. My past was painful to live through, but it did not happen without giving me a new purpose. Through it all, I firmly believe that God is in control of all things. I serve a God who makes beauty from ashes and beautiful things out of broken pieces. Through this journey, God began opening my eyes to a calling that I never imagined. It was only because of His grace that I was able to look back and remember things that I had previously blocked out. I urge you to hold fast in the knowledge that God is faithful and He has never left your side.

My journey is not over. I look back on everything that I went through and I wonder how I ever made it here. With each new day I have a better understanding of the strength that God has granted me to stay the course no matter the circumstances. He is always with me.

Looking Back

For you created my inmost being; you knit me
together in my mother's womb.

(Psalms 139:13)

*Dear Diary—today was a really good day. My
boyfriend bought me a carnation and he came
over after church for the afternoon.*

—journal entry, April 11, 1993

I want to encourage you to take a few minutes in the near
future to bring yourself back to your deepest hurt. Can you
remember the first time that you experienced something
painful?

When I was twenty-nine years old, I went through one
of the most difficult years of my life. I was navigating my
way through a divorce that felt like the end of everything
God had intended for me. I believe that God wants what is
very best for us, and I also believe that Satan, God's enemy
and our enemy, is doing everything possible to prevent that
from happening. I know that the enemy has tried to con-
vince me to tuck away the great pain that my heart endured
during different seasons for many years. Through some
unexpected, but miraculous recent obstacles, God has

helped me to reopen those dark places in my life and He continues to lead me to the truth so that I can help others who may be struggling with the same kind of hurt. I have begun to feel a true healing take place where before I was so weak and vulnerable. By revisiting my past and facing it head-on, I have begun to understand who I am and more of the purpose for which I was created.

Over the course of writing this book, I struggled many times with what to share in regard to these painful chapters in my life. I have no desire to bring any hurt to my children or to anyone else. I recognize that this is just my story and that we all have one we can tell. In telling my story I have no intention of dragging anyone else down, but I believe that sweeping things under the rug has controlled my life for long enough. I choose to live free from that. Thankfully this is a choice that I can control.

I was born on July 7th, 1977 at 4:44 p.m. 7/7/77 at 4:44.

When I take the time to reflect on my childhood, I am uncertain if all my memories are accurate or not. I have tried to think back to my earliest recollection of pain. I cannot remember anything occurring that was very traumatic, at least not serious enough to tamper with my emotions, until I became a teenager. I know that our family lost a dog when I was around five or six and that her name was Babes; she was hit by a car. I have a vague memory of that night being dark, lonely, and sad for me while I sat and watched TV in the basement of our small A-frame home. I do not really remember having a deep connection with our dog because we had not had her for very long.

I remember praying and asking Jesus to come into my heart when I was around five years old. I remember being at the church with my dad one day and I remember him talking with me about the questions that I had regarding Jesus. I was baptized the next Sunday.

My parents bought a video camera when I was around eleven and I now wonder if re-watching our home videos has altered my childhood memories. I wonder if the funny young girl in front of the camera was acting or not. I think the tapes caught my true personality. It seems as though I was not afraid of the camera and that I quickly learned how to get a laugh from those in the room and from the one behind the lens.

I was the second child in our family of six. My dad was a fiery Baptist pastor filled with passion, and my mother was a sweet soft-spoken woman of God with amazing faith. Together they had a strong desire to raise a family who loved each other and the Lord, and they wanted the world to see that family.

I had a brother almost two years older than me, and then a younger sister two years after me. We also had two younger brothers, one of whom died from Sudden Infant Death Syndrome when I was three and a half.

The fact that we were homeschooled for a few years and that I wasn't able to wear pants does stand out in my mind. Because we were homeschooled, our family was incredibly close. My siblings and I learned to defend and love one another, and we built strong relationships during our elementary years. We were able to take family field trips together and many of my favorite memories come from this time.

My 6th grade year, my parents decided to send us to a Christian school. Some of the families that attended this school also held the same standards my family did, so I was able to make the adjustment well. I know that having my siblings there with me helped in the process of fitting in. But by the end of that school year we learned that the school was not offering a high school for the following year, which meant we had to find another school. My parents decided to transfer us to another Christian school, which was also a Baptist school, so again the transition seemed pretty normal for me. Not only did I have my siblings with me, but also half of my previous school made the switch. As I prepared to start my 7th grade year, I know that my interest in boys became stronger.

At our new school there was a dress code that followed the same standards my family embraced, so I felt "the same" as the girls that I went to school with. I didn't stand out for any particular reason.

Everything changed in 8th grade. The school adopted a new policy that allowed girls to wear pants to school. I remember feeling different and wanting to be the same as everyone else. This is when I began to understand hurt. No one ever said anything to me about my not wearing pants, but I was sure they noticed, and so I began to revert and hide my feelings. I knew that my parents loved me and that they wanted the very best for me so I continued to strive to understand their reasoning for this conviction. It was just something that was not talked about in our home. It was my father's rule, so I knew that I needed to respect and submit to him as my authority. I wanted to have the right heart about this matter.

Not being able to wear pants was not the only rule in our lives. The school that I attended also embraced many of the same dos and don'ts that my parents followed and so the checklist of measuring-up began very early. A short list of the rules we lived by: no movies, no dancing, no drinking, no smoking, no sex, no rock music, no dating an unbeliever, and no swearing. Everything seemed black and white. There was no gray area. My parents probably had good Biblical reasons for each of these rules, but I don't remember the explanations for why we weren't allowed to do these things; I just know that the feeling of defeat swept in before I even had a chance to try. I had a desire to try all of them and that made me feel like I must be really bad.

When I entered my teenage years, I wanted to find love more than anything. Although I was receiving it at home, I also saw other teenagers holding hands. I think I had a different crush every week. My first few diaries would confirm that.

Even though I had begun to desire for a relationship, I know that by thirteen I still had not learned what "sex" meant. I was a very shy girl when it came to anything that seemed uncomfortable to talk about, so a conversation about something like this probably would have made me run away. Eventually, a friend of mine told me about sex one night when she stayed over.

During the next few years, I had little crushes on neighborhood boys and coworkers. I wrote down a new last name for myself on a piece of paper with my love of the week. I tallied up the "True Love" scores, which one of my friends had taught me how to do whenever I started liking someone new. I mean, if anyone understood love it was me. At least that's what I believed in my head.

When I was fifteen, I fell head over heels for a young boy that I had met in my youth group. My dad thought that maybe some one-on-one time with me would help me understand that there would be a future outside of my current crush. My dad and I went away together for the weekend, and we had some good conversations while we were gone. We drove a few hours away to walk around the campus of a nearby Christian college and to visit some family on that side of the state. My parents had met on a similar campus many years before.

We were only gone for a few nights but I do remember wanting to make the right choices after that. I knew the life that I wanted to have one day required making the right decisions along the way. It was a wonderful trip and shortly after we returned home, my dad gave me a beautiful purity necklace. I wore it around my neck with pride.

Shortly after this visit, my father reconsidered his dress code and let me know that I could now wear pants if I wanted to. I had been begging for this change, and he saw my hurt and responded to it during a conversation with me in our family's living room. With tears in his eyes, my father told me that I was more important to him than any rule. I saw his heart that night and it helped me understand that this conviction of his was deeper than I knew and rooted in love. The problem is that I was already set on a course of rebelling against a list that I couldn't measure up against. Although I was now allowed to wear pants, I also wanted to try all the other things that were forbidden.

I had just started working for a restaurant in town where I had met people that did all the things that I had been raised to believe were wrong. They swore, drank, smoked, had sex, danced, went to movies, and listened to rock music. But they were also nice and fun and accepting of me too. They had no lists to follow and I liked it.

My church boyfriend and I broke up after dating for a year. We had grown more promiscuous, and I felt tainted. I wanted to do the right thing. I really did. I ended up dating another boy for a short period of time, only to have it end with another broken heart.

During the end of my junior year of high school, my manager at the restaurant would often hit on me in a way that made me feel uncomfortable. He was much older than me and married, and I remember feeling very confused about my feelings toward him. I knew that I shouldn't like him, but I was also flattered by his attraction toward me because I was so much younger than he was. His flirtatious behavior really altered my understanding of reality. This twisted relationship played with my mind and carried on for months.

In the first few weeks of my senior year, a high-school friend and I went to visit another friend at her college in Ohio. During that visit, I met a young man from Chicago. He had a desire to serve the Lord and he was interested in me. I told my parents about him. At first, they were resistant because of his age but after he came to our home for a visit, they did allow us to begin dating. He commuted back and forth to visit me and I did the same. I told him about the predator from my work, although I didn't use that word then. He seemed surprised, and he encouraged me to stand up for myself. I remember quickly ending the secret relationship that had formed with my manager once I started dating my new boyfriend. I felt a new sense of power following that conversation, and I never really spoke of this situation again for years to come.

My family grew to like my new boyfriend more and more, and we started talking about marriage even though I was still in my senior year of high school. Although I thought I was ready, it also created a great fear inside of me. I think that the shame from my last relationship needed to be dealt with.

When I visited my boyfriend in Chicago, we spent time with some of his old friends. They lived a rough life.

He and I would go to church when we were together, but an attraction to life outside of the church was inviting too.

The summer after I graduated, I began making arrangements to get an apartment with a girl who had also graduated from my school. I was making decent money at the restaurant and feeling independent. I had opened up my own checking and savings account and had developed good financial discipline by depositing the money that I was making. I began to build up my bank account and purchase things for our new apartment.

I knew that my boyfriend was disappointed that I was choosing to not go to college, and I didn't like that I was letting him down. After he went back to school in the fall, the idea of a long-distance relationship with him became too difficult to think about, so I started to give up. I was scheduled to get my new place on October 12th, 1995, and I was busy buying furniture and collecting decorations while dreaming of not having any rules.

I remember going out for pizza one night with friends. I heard someone say Kyle's name. Kyle was a boy who had been in my class my 6th grade year. His family had moved away that same year, and I heard that they had all recently moved back to town. I remember wondering how he was doing and I found myself asking questions that night about him.

Just a few weeks later, I attended his sister's wedding, where she married my cousin. I knew Kyle would be there.

Moving Out

And a highway will be there; it will be called the Way
of Holiness; it will be for those who walk on that
Way. The unclean will not journey on it; wicked fools
will not go about on it.

(Isaiah 35:8)

*So much is changing. I am graduated now and
getting my own apartment in about a month. I
can't wait to decorate it. I may go to college, but
not yet. I am making good money at work.*

—journal entry, August 25, 1995

When I walked into the church for the wedding, I saw him
almost right away. Kyle looked so different than I remem-
bered. He had long hair now and even wore a marijuana
leaf necklace around his neck. I walked over to say hello,
and we exchanged a few words. I remember feeling per-
plexed during the wedding. I was drawn to this old friend,
but he was also a mystery to me. After the wedding, I stood
outside with the other guests as we waited for the bride and
groom. Afterward, he asked me for a ride home and wondered if I wanted to hang out for the afternoon. I said yes.
The house that he lived in oozed with sadness. I could feel
the pain through the living room walls. I had to work just

a few hours later so I wasn't planning to stay long. I don't remember much of our conversation that afternoon. I am sure I told him about my boyfriend and the new apartment that I was getting. I remember a green triple chamber water bong that was poorly hidden in the corner. I had never seen one before and I didn't know what it was for. A few minutes later, he was packing it with something that looked like shredded grass. He pulled out his lighter, lit the bong, and inhaled. I copied him. I don't really remember much after that point.

I believe I went to work a few hours later. I know that I talked to friends at work about having a new place to hang out for that night. I knew that I shouldn't go back, but I did. I invited my soon-to-be-roommate to come along with me too. I lied to my parents about where I'd be staying, even though I had church in the morning. I think I drank that night, I am pretty sure I smoked again from that same bong. I know there were a lot of people there and that I wasn't in control of my thoughts.

My boyfriend came home from college the next weekend to see me and I broke our relationship off. I wanted more of this new drug that was in my system. I'd already been back a few times for more. I liked how it made me feel numb, and I could get rid of the guilt that came the next morning as soon as I smoked it again. A few weeks later, my roommate and I received the keys for our new place. She had also found some new friends who were doing the same types of things I was.

Our new apartment would never become what we had first set out for it to be. We kept making the same choices every night. Every time we would hang out with our new friends, we would meet more of the same kind of people. The time while I lived in this apartment went by so fast and feels like a dream. I have few details left in my mind of the short few months. Every day until the following spring, I would be high.

Kyle, my reunited friend, became my boyfriend, and he moved in to live with me at my new apartment. I remember a few conversations with my older brother that revealed the extent of the pain that I was causing my family.

I would continue to go to church every Sunday, because something in my heart told me to keep going. I don't remember a single message during that season, but I know that God was speaking to me. I do remember the guilt because it was so strong. I know that I didn't want this for my life anymore, but I didn't know how to stop. There were so many people and things that would have to be taken out of my life in order for the change to happen, and I felt as though I couldn't crawl out of this hole that I had made with my life. It was so much easier to just light the new little pipe that now lived in our apartment. If I did that, then I would forget the mess that I had gotten myself in. I can remember some of the music that I was listening to around that time. The lyrics were sad and I felt as though I could relate to the artists who wrote them.

I know that I wanted to share my faith with the new

friends that I was meeting and I tried to sometimes. I can only imagine how silly I must have sounded and looked. They didn't understand the complete contrast between the two worlds that I was living. I knew that I had a loving family just a few miles away and that they were praying for me too. One of my phone calls home to my brother produced a "family talk" where I shared with them that I was addicted to marijuana. They were concerned and wanted to help. I remember letting my parents back into my world and knowing that I couldn't do this without them.

The marijuana clouded my mind and filled my life with so much confusion. The days and nights from that season all blend together. I was sexually active while I was smoking this drug. I didn't really care about myself anymore. I don't remember thinking of the possibility of getting pregnant but I'm sure that it did enter my mind. I remember having a weird craving for some kind of food one night at work and I remember someone saying, "Are you sure you aren't pregnant." It was the first time that the thought had occurred to me. I bought a pregnancy test that same night. It was positive, and I remember feeling relieved because I knew that this would cause me to change my lifestyle. My mom was the first person that I called. She told my dad after our phone conversation, and I knew they would extend grace to us.

My father was a minister, and his daughter had fallen into sin. What would others think? My boyfriend and I met with my dad at his office to discuss the situation that we were in. He offered us support and council and wondered how we felt about marriage. He also wanted to know if we loved each other and were planning to spend our future together. I remember hoping that Kyle would want to marry me. We discussed what that might look like and we scheduled a date for a wedding.

As we began planning the wedding, I had hope for my future again. I packed up my apartment and moved back home with my family. I remember reconnecting with my sister and wanting to be a good influence on her. I began to fall in love with my growing belly and the anticipation of becoming a wife and mother. A few weeks later my fiancé and I sat in the pews of my father's church while he told the congregation of our situation. There was one man whose response I worried about the most. He was my father's right hand man and the head deacon of our church, and a grandfather figure to me. He stood up and recited a reference from John chapter eight in the Bible; it is the chapter that talks about the woman caught in the act of adultery. Jesus' words were, "Anyone who has no sin let them speak up". That was all that was said.

My shame was over and we were embraced with open and loving arms from the whole congregation. The church threw us a baby shower and my fiancé and I began attending services together.

I looked at this precious baby growing inside of me as a gift from God. I had an instant burden to protect the baby and to give it a beautiful life like I had known.

Building a Family

But if serving the LORD seems undesirable to you,
then choose for yourselves this day whom you
will serve, whether the gods your ancestors served
beyond the Euphrates, or the gods of the Amorites,
in whose land you are living. But as for me and my
household, we will serve the LORD.

(Joshua 24:15)

*The sun is shining. The birds are chirping and I
have high spirits. I want to be in God's will, to
seek His face. But there are so many distractions
of everyday life that get in the way. I want God's
love to shine through me.*

—*journal entry, March 24, 2000*

I smiled a lot the summer day of our wedding. I wore
white. We sang "It Takes 3," a song about our marriage
needing the two of us and God to make it work. I was just
eighteen years old and saying "I do" for the rest of my life
to someone that I hardly even knew.

We bought a home, painted a baby room, and started
to become a family. I attended my first women's retreat with
my mother at Lake Ann Camp, and our relationship began
to mend. I saw her differently now. I needed her wisdom,

and I wanted to become like her. I remember the ladies in our retreat group pouring their Godly wisdom into me. I'm sure they could sense my hunger for God. Looking back, I see that this is when God began pruning me to become who He had created me to be. Anthony Blare made his way into our world a few months later and my life was forever changed.

This business of following Christ wasn't easy. Although I had heard all of the stories many times before, I was now reading them by myself for the first time and they brought an excitement to my spirit. I went back to work at the restaurant after having my son, and I was a different person. I wanted to talk with my coworkers about what I was reading and the truths that I was discovering. It was like I had just discovered something that was brand new, and I thought others would want to hear it. Little by little, I was losing my old friends. I knew that God was doing something in me and I liked how it made me feel about myself. I began to journal again. I was also drawn to the Christian radio station instead of the other stations that I had once listened to. When we would hang out with our friends, I participated in the drinking , but I kept feeling like I wanted to focus our conversation toward spiritual things. I felt compelled to talk about Jesus and how He was changing my life. We continued to go to church as a family, and we met new friends there. Some of them are still my good friends today.

Within two and half years, we were pregnant again.

At the ultrasound, I found out that we were having twin boys. It was very exciting news. What a miracle. We began to plan and do some house rearranging. We needed two of everything, and God provided for all of our needs.

I remember a conversation where my husband very innocently said that I was going to get "so big" while being pregnant for twins. I know that he was not saying it to hurt me, it was just a fact; I was pregnant with twins. That was the first time I remember worrying about my weight. I'm sure that I had thought about it before that day. I know that I often weighed myself while I was in high school, but I had never told myself to not eat or to obsess about it like I soon would.

My husband and I were having financial problems during the summer of the pregnancy, and he chose to leave me for a few nights because of the pressure. I felt panic sink into my world. This abandonment added to my worries about gaining weight and the future of our family. I associated my looks with being lovable. I knew that I had to eat for the boys and I was hungry, but I didn't want to gain weight. I was still so young and now I was pregnant with my second and third children. The thought of having to raise them all by myself was a great fear.

I'm not sure if I watched a program on bulimia or where the idea came from, but I remember I began to sneak into the bathroom frequently after I ate in order to purge. Once I tried it, I realized it worked for me and I knew that nobody would have to know. I read somewhere that when you are pregnant your child eats all that they need in the first few minutes after you eat. So I felt okay with my new routine. I would eat and eat and eat, and then I would wait for three minutes and go stick my finger down my throat in the bathroom. I told people that I was "sick." I even told people that it was really common to be sick the whole pregnancy with twins. I think I even tried to trick myself into believing that this was just a pregnancy thing, even though I was the one sticking my finger down my throat.

Once things were going better in the marriage, I justified my eating disorder because I thought that I would stop after I delivered the babies. The fear of getting "fat" drove me every day. This sin and stronghold in my life stole my joy and created fear and guilt. It controlled so much of my life and nobody knew that it was even a struggle for me. I felt stuck in a cycle that I knew I needed to stop, and I thought that the birth of the twins would produce the cure I longed for.

We bought a minivan, I turned twenty-two, and just over a month later, David Wayne and Andrew Jon were born healthy at five pounds each and six weeks early. These two bundles of joy were yet another gift from God Himself. He had protected them in the womb from my eating disorder. God blessed me beyond what I could have ever asked for in my life by giving me three healthy and beautiful children. I was created to be a mother.

Once the twins were born, I was too busy and tired to

eat in the first few weeks so I thought that maybe my eating disorder was gone. The eight pounds that I did gain during the pregnancy diminished and more weight continued to shed. I weighed ninety pounds just a week after the boys were born. I was weak and dehydrated, but the disorder made me feel victorious. Here I needed to be healthy to take care of our three children, but I was now controlled by the size of pants I could wear. I knew that it was dysfunctional, but I believed that I was still in control of this situation, and that led me to keep my disorder a secret.

Childcare expenses prevented me from being able to work, which presented a bigger need for me to cry out to God. I know that the first few years after the twins were born I stayed home almost every day by myself. There weren't very many places that I could take all of the boys without help, not even to the grocery store. I remember my small kitchen in our home. The window was located just next to the chair that I sat in each morning during the boy's naptime. It was in that small kitchen that I learned to hear from God for the first time. The sun would stream in and warm my shoulder and face, and I could feel His touch. It was there in that chair that I learned to trust Him with my daily needs and to rely on Him for providing for our home.

For many years, I continued to struggle with my eating disorder. There were times when life within my marriage would get tough, and then the vicious cycle would start back up again. I slowly realized I wasn't in control of it, but I still couldn't reach out for help due to the shame that

I carried from it. It no longer gave me the results that I was first able to get from purging. In fact, now I would get stomachaches and I was gaining weight instead of losing it.

The depression consumed me. I hated it now. I kept telling myself that I could stop. I was able to do that as long as everything in my life was in order, but if I started to see myself losing control of circumstances around me, that was when I needed a fix. I needed something to make it go away and let me feel in control again. Although I knew it wasn't taking my problems away, it had been my coping mechanism for many years now.

I reached out to my mom and sister at a women's retreat one year. I remember their concern for me and their determination to walk with me to face it and to seek professional help. I spoke of this secret in my life so openly now to them for the first time, and I knew that they were going to be asking me about it. I wouldn't be able to hide it from them any longer.

I would like to say that I was cured after that weekend retreat. I know that my speaking up and having others know of my struggle was huge, but I was going to have to be the one to choose to stop the cycle myself. I needed God to show me who I really was "in Him". I didn't understand my true identity for so long. I know that He was showing me and I am so thankful that over time I was able to realize that neither my pant size nor the number on the scale changed anything about who I was. I needed internal healing and He was listening.

I have been completely healed of this disease since the year 2005. I give God all the glory for delivering me from the bondage that I once had from it.

> But thanks be to God! He gives us the victory
> through our Lord Jesus Christ.

>   (I Corinthians 15:57)

The Wind Blows

The rain came down, the streams rose, and the winds blew and beat against that house, and it fell with a great crash.

(Matthew 7:27)

Lord, I beg of you for a friend that will strength-en me and encourage me to stay strong.

—journal entry, November 20, 2001

My marriage spent most of its years in a difficult place. Neither my husband nor I had gone to college, so the ability to support a family of five was very difficult. We were so young and there was great pressure from every side. God would bless us and then a new obstacle would come. It seemed like a roller coaster.

In 2001, we sold our home and found a big, beautiful new home to buy on a land contract. It just finally felt "right." Our oldest son was now in school and the twins were toddlers. We had a strong young adult ministry forming at church and many new friends.

I knew that I needed a good friend to help me stay the course that the Lord was calling me to follow. Just a month after I wrote about this desire in my journal, I hosted a jewelry party at my house for Tana, a jewelry consultant. The day we finalized the order, she came over to sit with me to go through the paperwork together.

We got along really well, and then hung out a few times after that. She and her husband began to have marital problems, so she decided to live with some friends while they were separated. A few months later, she returned to Muskegon to work things out after she found out that she was pregnant. They began to look for a new church to attend, so I encouraged them to come with us. We started hanging out with Tana and her husband on a regular basis. Her and I talked about doing a daycare together so we decided to put an ad in the paper and quickly landed our first child.

We were very excited about working together during the day as God had been strengthening our friendship during our time spent together.

Shortly after we started the business, her husband left her again for someone else. My heart broke for her. She would come over to help me watch the kids during the day and I could sense her loneliness and desperation for God to fix things. I wanted to offer the right words to her although I didn't know what to say. I feared that my own marriage was unraveling again, and I had an incredible amount of fear that I would end up in the same boat that Tana was in. Her failing marriage touched a real fear in my life because I understood the pain from my past separations with Kyle. I wanted to be a supportive friend and my heart was breaking for her. She moved out of her house and back home with her parents, because being alone was too painful for her.

With our new home, our bills had increased and there was more pressure on us. I think my husband felt trapped. I don't think he knew what to do, and he often dealt with the pressure by leaving. I said hurtful things to him that probably made him feel like he wasn't good enough for me as a husband and provider. After Tana moved out of her house, her husband moved back into it by himself. My husband decided to live there with him and share the rent.

By the end of the first week of Kyle being gone, I knew that it was different this time. He'd left for a night or two before, but this time it really seemed like it was going to be the end of our marriage.

I had to pack up everything and say goodbye to the house that we were buying on land contract. We had only been there for six short months before the boys and I moved in with my parents. The Lord knew just how much I was going to need a friend like Tana to stay encouraged through the new storm in my path. We talked every night on the phone. The last thing we would say to each other was, "Ask God to hold you in His palm." He always would.

Our parents watched our kids for us so we could still attend our Saturday night Bible studies. My dad bought me a guitar and taught me a few chords on it. After the boys went to bed, I would sit and strum and come up with words to give expression to what I was feeling. I wrote a few songs, and my children and parents would play audience for me. They were so supportive. My dad even invited me to join him on the praise team at church. He believed in me.

> *"My heart is aching. I can hardly even move. I'm so broken Lord—what are you trying to teach me? What is happening? Lord, my Rock, lift me up to the heavens and cover me with your love. Fill me! Place your arms around me and help me to shine and soar during this deep agony. Show me your complete reason for why I am here today going through this. Prepare me for my next steps. May I not even breathe on my own. I want to know you more God."*
> —journal entry, July 12, 2002

As the months passed, God was bringing His healing. My husband and I talked a few times, and he let me know that he continued to want to be separated from me. We agreed for him to have the boys for a few hours one night a week and every other weekend. He and I barely talked during our months of separation. He had found new friends and a new life outside of me.

I registered for nurse aide classes and prayed about what to do with my future. I filed for a legal separation and for child support. I actually went to the courthouse one day to also file for a divorce. I prayed for clarity the whole ride there and pulled up to find that the courthouse was closed for the day. There had been a bomb threat that morning, so I marched back to my car with a clear confirmation from the Lord. One month later, I drove there again praying the same prayer, and this time I was able to walk in and leave with the signed papers from a judge. Our divorce was now in process. I felt a sense of closure and some anticipation for my future. It had been five months since we'd been together and I was forming a new life outside of Kyle. The pain was less intense and I felt free to release our marriage over to the Lord.

> *"Memories, memories. I'm losing them.*
> *Sometimes I catch myself being me (the*
> *wife) and loving it, baking and stuff. I just*
> *want to pretend that it's still me but it's*
> *not . . . Fall is deeper and deeper here."*
> —journal entry, September 22, 2002

My parents were an amazing source of strength for my boys and me. They recognized when I needed a few minutes to myself. They would step in to protect my boys. My dad would read to them each night and together we all had family devotions. I enjoyed becoming creative in making us all dinner while I was home during the day. The boys adjusted to the change well.

Every night before bed, the boys and I would pray for

their daddy. Whenever we were all in the car together, we would ask God to appear to us in the sky. I can remember times that the sky would have giant puffy clouds and then areas with small openings. We called those openings God's eyes. It became a coping mechanism for me to dream and imagine God being with us, and He was. One day about two weeks before Christmas, I was doing a project at our church and the phone rang for me. It was Kyle. He said he wanted to talk and he asked if he could come see me at the church. That afternoon, he walked in the church doors for the first time in six months, and I knew something was different.

Later that day, I remember driving out of the church parking lot and following him in the car ahead of us. My oldest boy said, "See, Mom, God was listening. We just needed to wait." We all looked out the window for a glimpse of God in the clouds. We knew that the Almighty had just visited us and we were looking for a quick glimpse of Him.

We were right. Kyle seemed happy. It felt so natural to reconcile, and almost immediately the kids and I moved in with him at his new place. Tana's divorce had finalized by now and her ex-husband moved out of the house that he and Kyle had shared. So now our family began to live in Tana's old home. We spent Christmas together as a family that year. I dismissed the court order for child support and recanted the divorce that was in process. I finished my nurse aide classes and landed a good job at a nursing home taking care of the elderly. Kyle decided to go back to school to get a college degree. We both began to work part-time and attend school. We worked around each other's schedules to make it work for our family.

With Tana's divorce now finalized she moved on with her life. We remained good friends but things in our lives were now different and it created division between us. I understood her distance; I couldn't imagine how hard it would have been for her to come over to visit me now as I was living in her old home. I wanted the friendship that we had once had, but it was too hard for us both. I felt as though I had to let her go so she could move on with her life and it was hard for me because she was such an encouragement and support to me for so long.

We didn't live in that house for very long, though. We got a loan and bought our next home in the spring of 2004.

The next summer I could sense some restlessness again in my marriage. I felt him withdrawing and becoming distant from me. He seemed stressed and extra irritable.

June 8, 2005 was our ninth anniversary. I was scheduled to work that morning, but then I was called off. I spent the day at the beach with the boys. We had prayer group later that night and I could not get ahold of Kyle on his cell phone. My heart had grown weary by the time I received a phone call later that night. Kyle said he wanted to let me move on with my life. He said I deserved better. He was sorry. I was confused beyond belief. I couldn't understand the self-hatred that caused him to push me out of his life. He shut down and withdrew. I hadn't understood it before, and I couldn't understand it now.

I thought again that this was the end of my marriage. Words cannot articulate the depth of my hurt. It was indescribable. I cried out to God, but I was also so angry with Him, too. I felt critically wounded yet I had to make important decisions and function because life does not stop when we're hurting. I remember being at a stop sign and feeling like I was in a dream. I just could not understand how the rest of the world was carrying on as if nothing had happened. I was attending a funeral in my heart and the cars were driving past me to get to their next destination.

I had no idea what we were going to do. I wanted to tell everybody I knew, and yet I also wanted to keep it private. We had just bought another new home. He only had one year left of school. We were finally "arriving." How could this be happening again? We both hurt so much, and that pain was creating more hurt now. I took the boys to stay at my parent's house many nights. Staying home with them on my own was too painful. My youngest brother and his wife, Sara, lived in the house next door to my parents, and I went up to visit them often. Sara cared for the boys while I had to work.

As the summer came to an end, I realized the boys needed structure again. They would be starting school in a week. The best and easiest thing to do was work things out with my husband. We needed counseling so badly, but we did not make it a priority. I don't think we realized the help that speaking up could have brought. I told myself that we could get through this with hard work, but I made a promise to myself that I would never go through this again. My heart would not endure another time through this process. Kyle and I talked, and he agreed to move back in before the boys returned to school that fall.

The next year we celebrated ten years of marriage with a trip to Punta Cana in the Dominican Republic. He finished school. The hurt in our past was still there, but we were moving forward. I signed up for business classes at a local college. I wrote a very detailed list that described the kind of job that I thought would be best for our family and for me, and I tucked it away in my Bible. The twins were now in school for full days, and I felt it may be time for me to explore the business realm and full-time work. God was faithful and I landed the job that He had waiting for me. I pulled out my detailed list to see what I had written down, and wasn't at all surprised that it mirrored my new job completely. I framed that list and placed it next to my computer on my new desk. Every day I could remind myself that God had heard my prayer.

But even though so many things were wonderful, I felt the discontent within him again.

> *"Lord, it's happening again . . . Please protect*
> *my children and my heart if he leaves again.*
> *I will know Lord that you are in control if he*
> *walks away, and I will trust in you to take care*

of the boys, my fears, my heart, my credit, our future, what people will say, who all this will affect. I know you're listening."

—journal entry, March 1, 2007

The next morning at work, I had my ninety-day review and I received a raise. The boys were with my parents for the night, and Kyle and I were supposed to have the night to ourselves. We had a powerful conversation in front of our fireplace where I asked him to let me into his heart. He said he couldn't. I told him that I could feel him pulling away again, and he said he didn't know what else I wanted from him. He walked out the door again and spent the night at a hotel.

I fell face-first onto the ground and poured my heart out to God, crying for an hour. I finally realized that he was not coming back. I could not understand it. But I knew that I had to move forward. After struggling for ten years in our marriage, I felt the release and had Biblical grounds now to file for a divorce and I chose to pursue that and never looked back.

Part of My Roots

How good and pleasant it is when God's people live
together in unity.

(Psalms 133:1)

*So much is going on. We finally got the church
plant with my brother Jerry up and running.
We had about 50 people there on our opening
Sunday last week. I am growing spiritually and
I really hope it continues. I am thankful for all
that God has blessed us with.*

—*journal entry, March 12, 2005*

In order to give you a better understanding of my story, I
want to go back to some key points that have shaped who I
am still becoming.

I have always looked up to my older brother, Jerry. We
were just under two years apart, and I valued anything that
he liked. I remember him visiting after my oldest son was
born, and I could see the desire in his eyes to have a family
for himself. He hated being alone, just like I had, and
wanted so desperately to find someone to have and to hold.

Because I was his younger sister and I was already
living the life he was pursuing, I hurt for him and his

longing. Just a few weeks after the twins were born, he and I rode together to pick up a girl that he'd just started dating. I could sense the intense emotions that he felt for her already, so I was naturally excited to meet her. Jamie Jo was the perfect woman for my brother, absolutely perfect in every way. Not just anyone could fit into our crazy family. It would take a very special young lady to measure up to all of the standards that Jerry desired in his future bride. You see, he had my mother as an example for what a woman should be. It would be very difficult to find someone that could compare to her.

I remember watching them fall in love that fall. It felt so good to finally see my brother get what he'd wanted for so long. A very strong woman of faith and she was also under five feet tall. We come from a short family. His proposal was on the front page of the local paper, and their wedding day was shared with friends from all over.

Jerry had a burning desire to change our world. He and I both saw the same passion in our father, so it was only natural that Jerry mimicked our father's drive to succeed in the vision God had given him. While Jerry and Jamie were still dating, they began a Bible study for young adults in the home that he was renting. I was lucky enough to be one of the ones that attended. I remember this as a real molding time in my relationship with Christ. I remember dreaming of becoming a church with the others who were attending our study. We all partook in fellowship and scripture, and always ended our time together with a very intimate setting of worship. The scriptures were becoming meaningful to me and I was beginning to see God transforming my heart for Him. My husband attended these Bible studies with me, and he was usually the one leading the worship on his guitar. This group was also a big source of support for Kyle and I during our marital problems.

In late 2004, after years of hosting Bible studies together and witnessing God shape this body of believers, we launched our first church. Jerry was the pastor and Kyle was the worship leader. Jerry and Jamie were now married and had their first daughter. We met in an old theater that had been recently renovated. It had a coffee bar in the entrance area. God also moved in the heart of a daycare center's owner—located right next door to our church—and she agreed to let us use her facility for our children's ministry.

As soon as the launch took place, our church community began to grow. The messages delivered more and more substance and lives were being changed each week. Our congregation was filled with young people and young families.

I can still remember a man named Jesus singing and clapping for joy in the front row. He had stage 4 cancer and was already supposed to be dead. He had a reason to sing and every once in a while he would get really excited and shout. When the worship had finished, Jerry would say something about why Jesus could celebrate so freely. The congregation understood and would respond with laughter and even give a clap of victory for him.

Having this church family and being in this place with my life began to feel "right" finally. I knew that this was the direction that God was leading me in and I enjoyed the process of being part of something that fit into a bigger picture. Although we had endured marital struggles in our past, the ones that were part of this body accepted us and carried their own wounds to the table too. The year of our divorce, they all carried the burden with us.

In the Storm

I will send down showers in season; there will be
showers of blessing.

(Ezekiel 34:26)

*The music's playing in the background, but
silence fills the house. I'm listening to it. The
pain is so fresh yet already beginning to fade.
Thoughts run through my mind . . . And then
the silence comes again. It's a quiet beauty in my
heart and soul.*

—*journal entry, March 14, 2007*

My desire to write about my journey is a recent passion.
When I first began writing my story, I would sometimes
wake in the night and find myself compelled to write more.
Memories and emotions were rolling around in my mind
as I was reminded of different times in my journey and of
my relationship with Christ. I wanted to be sure to retain
each of them. Looking back over my story, I was beginning
to see that He was with me in both simple and complex
ways.

The year of my divorce, I knew that I needed to press
forward and that healing would eventually come to my

heart. God did send different people to give me advice on how to understand this form of pain and the different emotions that it was going to bring. I came to understand that I could not skip the grieving stages that were ahead of me.

My brother, who was also still my pastor, suggested that I see a licensed counselor to help me process the pain. Our church paid for me to have six sessions with a counselor, and it felt so good to share my heart with someone who would give me professional advice. He suggested that I read a book called *Boundaries* by Henry Cloud and John Townsend. As I read through the first chapter of the book, I knew that the Lord was leading me to this wisdom. My counseling sessions, as well as the book, led me to understand the importance of establishing healthy boundaries within all of my relationships. The day of my last session with my counselor, the sun beamed and I finally caught a glimpse of hope for my future.

Spring soccer began again for the boys. The sidelines of the soccer field were always a place for me to be physically present with the boys during their practices while I allowed my emotions to flow into the journal lying in my lap. I captured almost every thought that I'd had for months. I wanted to retain what my heart was experiencing so that I had something to look back at when I was able to get to the other side of this pain.

One point of stability in our boy's life during this time of turmoil was their charter school. The teachers and staff rallied together for our boys, and they each played significant roles in filling the holes that had opened during this painful time. I am forever grateful for the staff and for the safe place that our boys were able to have each morning when they were dropped off.

One secret I had preserved during these years was the fact that I was a closet smoker. Cigarettes had been like a companion for me during this dark time, and I remember sitting outside at night—after I would put the boys to bed—with a cigarette in hand. I would talk out loud to the Creator of the universe, asking Him difficult questions about the season that I was in. And then I would whisper to myself the answers that I thought He would say if I could hear Him. He felt so far away yet so close too.

> The Lord is close to the brokenhearted and saves those who are crushed in spirit.
>
> (Psalms 34:18)

My journal during this time shows quotes and verses on each page of it. This one I had underlined:

> *"It is only God who can fill our deepest longings, who never has an appointment elsewhere, who never replaces us with someone He likes better, who promises never to leave us totally alone. He is the only one who wants to be and always can be the unfailing companion on our journey."*
>
> —Gini Andrews

As the anger stage of dealing with this grief sank in, I felt entitled to fall apart. I was angry, lonely, sad, and confused. Why was this happening? I felt like I had a huge, dark cloud hovering over my head, but I did not really want the cloud to go away because I was not quite sure what was going to be next for me and the boys. I wanted to absorb the hurt just a bit longer because I was not really ready to face accepting that this was even real. I was so afraid of truly letting go. All I had ever dreamed of was being married and having children, and that dream was falling apart for me. Why couldn't I have what everyone else seemed to have?

I made some poor decision during the first few months of the divorce process. I traveled down two roads for a time, losing myself in those choices. I hated being alone. I knew that God was in control but I was in such pain.

One Friday night when I did not have my boys, I went to a bonfire with my brother, Jerry, and his family. I remember sitting around the fire with a bunch of people that I did not really even know, sharing in the prayer and fellowship. I remember telling the people around the fire that night that I was hurting and that I was really questioning where God was in all of the things happening in my life.

Before Kyle left, I had been doing a study in my Bible about Jesus' name and the power that lies in His name alone. I had been praying that I would have an "eternal marriage" in the name of Jesus every day on my way to work in the weeks before he left—and yet h still left. I talked with them about the study that I had been doing and the anger that I was now feeling toward the Lord, because I felt like He hadn't been listening to me.

We all prayed together for the requests that were mentioned. Afterward two women I'd never met approached me to share their hearts with me. They told me to pray very specifically for God Almighty to begin to loose the chains that I was bound to in my marriage, in the Name of Jesus. I took in their words of wisdom and prayed intently that night as I fell asleep when I got home and a few times afterward when my heart was heavy with grief.

On July 10th, I had scheduled a prayer counseling session with a ministry that was dedicated to prayer and counseling. The ministry is structured to bring you back through past sins in your life and encourage steps of repentance and surrendering. It was a very powerful experience for me.

I drove to a house where some people were waiting for me. I sat on their back deck while looking over a pamphlet filled with scripture and questions for me to answer.

They came out to get me and led me into a sitting room in their beautiful house. I sat with these two women that would lead me to revisit some painful times from my past. We prayed over my past and I asked for forgiveness and healing for areas that I had forgotten about. The sun was beginning to set that night while I was driving home, and it was a beautiful light to behold. I drove down the highway with my sunroof open and my hand stretched out the window so I could catch the wind with my fingertips.

I turned the music up and began thanking God for the release of pain that I was experiencing. For the first time in months, I knew I was going to be okay.

As July moved on, it was getting easier for me to be home alone. I walked through every room of my home while holding a bowl of oil. In each room I placed my finger in the oil and marked a cross on every door as I prayed out loud for different things, sometimes for each of the boys and sometimes for myself. I prayed for His protection and faithfulness. I was committed to making my home a safe place for the boys. I desired for them to feel peace and freedom every time they entered our front door. I placed inspirational sayings and verses all around the house. The wall that led up to my bedroom was my favorite. I saved that wall for the cards that I knew I would need to read the most.

After five months, I finally didn't fear staying home at night without my boys. I spent some quiet nights with the Lord, and I remember singing loudly as I tried to learn a few Jennifer Knapp songs on my guitar. My need to have someone to talk with on the phone was diminishing and my journal entries were growing less frequent. I took early morning walks before work in my neighborhood with my friends Mary and Marcia, and they would listen to me ramble. They offered wonderful advice during that season and have continued to be great friends and wonderful sounding boards over the years.

One night while I was going through some old things,

I found the necklace that my dad had given me when I was sixteen. It had a locket in the shape of a heart. When I opened it, I found a gold heart inside. My dad had cut out a piece of pink paper in the shape of a heart and placed it in the locket. The paper said, "I love you." On the opposite side of the piece of paper, he wrote the date. I was so happy to find the necklace again, and I decided to hang it on the side post of my bed. For the first time in a long time I dreamed of giving my heart to someone again.

Although Tana had moved an hour away from me, our relationship remained strong. She was remarried and living a beautiful new life. She was supportive throughout the years and our friendship had developed deep roots. When she heard of my situation again, she called to check in on me. She invited me to visit her anytime I might need it. She also spoke with great wisdom and prayed with me often. She reminded me that God would hold me in His palm at night and that I wasn't alone.

> *"Another weekend is here. It's time to shine,*
> *God. Show me how to be used of you today.*
> *Give me a passion for souls. Use me as your*
> *servant. Cleanse my mind and help me to*
> *stand tall. My mission starts in the home*
> *with my boys. Help me to recognize this first.*
> *God, I beg you to have mercy on my boys. To*
> *start a wildfire in their hearts that can't be*
> *quenched."*
>
> —journal entry, July 20, 2007

On August 12th, 2007, I packed up my car and drove to a small lake in the area. It was a place that I knew would not be busy, and a place where I knew I could watch a beautiful sunset. I got out of my car and sat down on a blanket. The beach was empty that early evening. I saw some broken concrete near where I was sitting, and something told me to go over to it. I remember picking up some small rocks and talking to God out loud. I began crying and made new promises to God as I continued to release the pain of loneliness. The pile of rocks grew higher and higher. It was becoming an altar. I found two long sticks to form a cross to put on the top of it. I wrote the date in the sand and the words "I promise" and then I took a picture. I packed up my car and drove home.

The very next night, I was incredibly lonely and sad again. I was really struggling with the emptiness of being alone. It would come on so strong at night. I wanted to be loved so badly. I got out my note cards and wrote these words with a red marker:

> *"God, I beg you to take this loneliness I feel.*
> *This desire to be wanted and truly loved. I*
> *turn to you!"*
>
> —journal entry, August 13, 2007

I added it to the wall that led up to my bedroom. Then I pulled out a notebook and wrote a letter to God. On the opposite side of the letter I put together a detailed list for a future husband and I fell asleep peacefully—in His palm.

I received news the next morning that a young friend of mine named Mary had passed away. She was only twenty-nine years old, and had died from a brain aneurysm. When I told my coworkers about this situation, they were saddened to hear the shocking news. Our conversation at my desk was somber as I left for her visitation. I remember saying to them, "God never does anything without having a reason, even if it is just to change one person's life, there is always a plan."

I saw Eric Wagenmaker's name on the guestbook while I was signing my name in. The room was mostly quiet, aside from the video and song playing on a screen in the middle of the room. Eric came over and asked how I was doing. I knew he had heard about my once-again failed marriage, and I knew that was what he was asking about.

Eric was someone I had known since the 7th grade. His mom was my cheerleading coach for five years. His sister was one of my closest friends in high school. Eric had filled in to lead worship for my former husband when he'd stepped away from his position at the church during the summer of 2005. He had been very close to both of my brothers and in the same grade as my younger sister. He was also Mary's cousin—the girl who had passed. He was going through a difficult season too. His parents and his sister were going through divorces that same year.

Right in the midst of all this brokenness and grief, I knew God was here with me.

Rebuilding

"For I know the plans I have for you," declares the
LORD, "plans to prosper you and not to harm you,
plans to give you hope and a future."

(Jeremiah 29:11)

*I just went for a walk . . . the church bells are
ringing now. I'm sitting in the living room by myself with the windows open. It's Sunday morning.
I started talking to a guy named Eric recently.
I've known him since I was in high school and
our paths just crossed again.*

—journal entry, September 2, 2007

The next day some of us planned to get together after
Mary's funeral. I had the boys with me. I hoped that Eric
would be coming too. He came late that evening, just before the boys and I left.

The next day my sister, Janelle, called to tell me that
she had told him to call me sometime. She'd told him to
take me out for coffee. He'd stayed late to talk with Janelle
and her husband about where he was in his life and then to
listen to her share some of what God was doing in my life.

A few days later, Eric picked me up to go out for coffee.
I talked the whole time and he listened well. The follow-

ing week I went over to his house. While we were there, he played worship songs on his guitar while I flipped through a book that he had assembled after his recent missions stay in South Africa. I was smitten!

I could not believe that God could bring someone so amazing into my life. I was in awe of the power of God's grace. I went to see my parents a few days later and I cried tears of joy while I shared with them the thoughts of my future.

Was this from God?

Eric would now stand with me in my row at church while the boys were in their class. I remember that during worship Iclosed my eyes and listened to him sing songs of praise to our King. I had a reason for the smile on my face, and my hands rose high. My heart was merry again.

Even though I was overjoyed, I had some of the fears that any mother going through this would have: What about my boys? How will they handle this? When is it okay for him to be around them? How much is too much? I wanted to shout to the world that I was finding love again.

Eric had just stepped down from his position at a church to go on tour with a band. He would be leaving two weeks following our first coffee visit and would be gone for a month or more. Before he even left, our hearts were beginning to connect.

When he left for his trip, our phone conversations were meaningful and quickly took on the language of deepening our relationship when he returned. We had to work through the tough things that needed to be discussed in order for us to move forward in a relationship that would last. He had never been married and had no children of his own. It was important for him to know whether or not I wanted more children. I still remember how that question made me smile over the phone. His second big question was whether or not I would follow him into ministry. He said that he knew that he had a calling to lead worship. I started dreaming then of what we could become as a team.

When Eric finally made it back home I hosted a get-together at my house with church friends so he could come over while the boys were there. I watched him interact with each of them and I remember the nerves in my stomach. He brought his guitar and softly strummed familiar cho-ruses while sitting on the couch. I went into the kitchen to say a silent prayer of thanksgiving. A few weeks later, he came over for the first time without others around, and we had a serious talk with the boys. Eric needed to gain their respect, and the boys deserved to know the truth about who he was.

Our hearts were so excited about all of the changes happening. It was hard for me to gauge the right timing for all the things that we wanted in our future.

We bought books on blending a family and we went to some counseling sessions together. He came around a lot more often. We worked ourselves into a new family.

One night while I was lying in bed and journaling, I pulled out the necklace my dad had given me long ago;

I looked at the pink piece of paper that was now almost twenty years old. Something told me to turn it around, and I saw the date my dad had given it to me: October 5, 1993. My heart skipped a beat. October 5th is Eric's birthday.

In March, the boys and I moved back in with my parents, and we decided that Eric and a few roommates would take over the mortgage on my home. The first night at my parent's house, I set up a blog to write about this new chapter in my life. I was finally ready to share with the world my unfolding future.

The move was perfectly timed for the boys and me. It was springtime again. Another new season with some much-needed sunshine. I knew that I needed my parent's wisdom, support and encouragement.

On April 19th, 2008, a Saturday afternoon, Eric arranged for my sister, both sister-in-laws, and his sister to be together at the house. As we sat in the living room, a limo made its way up the road in front of the house. I knew something was up and, boy, was I right. Eric had very creatively and secretly planned for me to go on an amazing adventure that he put together flawlessly. It included a treasure map arranged as individual pieces and written as a poem. Each new piece of the map brought me to my next clue, some roses, and my next destination.

The girls rode with me as I received a massage, a manicure, a visit to the place of our first date, and then a stop where a CD contained my next clue. The CD was Eric himself singing to me a song that he had written about us.

At the end of the day, and now the final stop, the limo and the girls disappeared as I read my final clue. The clue told me to head down to the X marked in the sand at the bottom of a long stairway that led to the shore of Lake Michigan. Eric was waiting for me on the beach. He was bare foot, wearing khakis and a white dress shirt, and he held a small treasure chest in his hand. He got down on one knee and asked me to be his wife. He included my whole family and my best friend Tana and her new husband in the party that followed. My mom and dad topped it off with a beautiful cake. My sister-in-law, Sara, taped the whole day of events. I don't think I stopped smiling the entire afternoon or evening. It was like a beautiful dream unfolding. I felt so incredibly special and I was so thankful that my family and Tana were able to see my world turning around in this way. We began to plan our wedding.

God took care of my boys' hearts while they suffered through the divorce in their childhood. Both their father and I found new beginnings with individuals who'd never married nor had any children.

Eric and I married exactly one year after our first date. I felt like Cinderella. Our ceremony was so personal and creative. My husband is gifted at putting together events and he worked incredibly hard at making this day extra-special for us. He organized every detail down to what song would be playing when our grandparents walked down the center aisle. Our sisters, Tana, and my good friend Erin stood by my side as bridesmaids. Some of the bridesmaids stayed with me the night before the wedding at the family cottage where our reception would be held. I remember walking out into the backyard early the morning of my wedding day. There was huge white canopy that took up the space of the entire yard. The small lake that the cottage sits on was beautiful and calm that morning. It was a special day for me, and I wanted to be sure to start it out with my first love. He overwhelmed me with His presence.

A few hours later, I walked down the aisle to Coldplay's "Fix You." Eric's pastor married us, and both my brother and father played roles in the ceremony. One of my favorite parts of our ceremony was my brother's prayer for a new beginning as a family. The song "Be Thou My Vision" was sung and the entire wedding party and both sides of our immediate family came up on the stage to surround us with their hands held out while Jerry prayed.

Each of my boys walked down the aisle before I came out to a special tribute that I had prerecorded for them.

The reception was held under the canopy overlooking the lake. Lights strung inside made the space truly magical. Our colors were ivory and black with rose color accents. The dance floor sat in the middle of the tent, and the DJ encouraged the guests to applaud as we entered and danced our first dance as man and wife to Etta James' "At Last." We received a standing ovation.

Lightning filled the sky that night, but no rain was in sight.

The Church Split

My God, my God, why have you forsaken me? Why are you so far from saving me, so far from my cries of anguish?

(Psalms 22:1)

Spring is coming! Time change happened last night. I am going to Lakeshore for possibly the last time today. Very very sad! What a mess. God we just ask you to show us "where to next."

—journal entry, March 9, 2008

A few months before Eric proposed to me, my brother had been asked to step down as the pastor at Lakeshore Community Church. The church was less than three years old and already numbered around four hundred members.

I remember Eric telling me the news. He had just started working with the worship team and he was scheduled to lead in a few weeks. He said that the worship director had told him that something had come up and that Jerry wouldn't be preaching for a while. I remember walking into my church that first Sunday after Jerry stepped down. The walls were talking to me. I knew it would never be the same again. I remember hiding down a hallway and wanting to cry out of hurt and confusion. I realized that most people there already knew of my brother's failure. I walked with my head held high and received hugs from some I would never see again. My brother sat up front with Jamie and he spoke at the end of the service. He asked for privacy and time to heal.

The next week, my brother and his wife were permitted to come to church, but not to speak. He had written something to say to the congregation, but they would never hear his words. They came in late and Eric led us in worship that morning. That was our last service with the people that had become a family to us. A few weeks later, I remember there was going to be a "special service" hosted by other pastors in the area to lead the congregation and the elder board to answer questions that the very confused congregation had. I decided to go. After all, I was a member. I didn't feel God in that space, though. I remember seeing people there who were from other congregations.

The events that led to my brother's resignation were complicated and simple at the same time. He had messed up. He had met with someone for coffee and he chose to show her some inappropriate pictures that he had on his phone. We live in a very small town and so the rumors began to fly quickly. Gossip filled the churches and streets very fast and it became more and more evident that he would not be able to rebuild his life in our hometown.

I remember going to work and my friend coming over to me to alert me that it was in our local news paper. Front and center. Not only was the whole Christian community going to find out why he had been asked to step down, but now our whole community knew too. My employer allowed me to leave work early that day, and I drove straight over to my parent's house. My father was a pillar for our whole family, and he demonstrated how we should handle this difficult situation. He asked me to ride with him for the day. He and I went to visit a woman dying at the Hospice center. We sat with her and her family and sang a song. I wondered what this family would think of us after they read the newspaper that day. My dad didn't seem to even care. I know he was worried, but he held his composure for the rest of us to lean on like he always had before.

Five months after Eric and I got married, my brother would stand before a judge. The judge had letters from influential people who were in opposition of Jerry ever leading a church again. The judge was very hard on him that day. The courtroom was filled with every emotion. Jerry's good friend Justin had just moved here from New Jersey to work with him on rebuilding his life. We never suspected that Jerry would get any jail time. My mother and my sister-in-law didn't attend. If it had been up to my brother, none of us would have been there. He didn't want any of us to experience his pain as observers.

Jerry was sentenced to ninety days in jail and two years of probation. We were all in shock. I remember the tears rolling down my face and the numbness in my broken heart. I knew it would hit the papers again, and it did.

Another great article to read and it didn't matter if it would potentially hurt my father's church congregation just miles down the road. My dad and brother both share the same name.

I felt homeless. I didn't know who I could trust anymore in the church community. It was incredibly difficult to not let the boys know what had truly happened, but how could I hide it? They knew their uncle was in jail, but they didn't know why. They knew that we'd lost our church community, but they didn't know the difficult circumstances. Eric stepped in with strong shoulders and thought we should go back to his church. It was large enough for me to hide in and just far enough away that not everyone would know who I was. I often say that I would have never returned to church again after this experience if it weren't for Eric. Perhaps I would have found my way back to a church on my own, but I do occasionally wonder what would have happened if I had not had Eric during this painful time.

Three months later, when my brother was released from jail, things would never be the same. Jerry knew he would have to move in order to limit the amount of pain this had brought on his family. One of my best friends and sister-in-law, Jamie, who had been with me through so much would now have to move away. My brother, one of my heroes, would not walk with me any longer. As I grieved this new loss, they began to search for new communities where they could start over.

Happily Ever After
(I Think)

See, I am doing a new thing! Now it springs up; do
you not perceive it? I am making a way in the wilder-
ness and streams in the wasteland.

(Isaiah 43:19)

Use me, Lord! That's my cry today. I know, God,
that you have brought me through so many
things and I just want to share with the world the
power of your provision through each trial.

—*journal entry, April 17, 2009*

Eric and I hung a plaque that read "And They Lived Hap-
pily Every After" in our bedroom. It was one of our wedding gifts. We'd had a beautiful time on our honeymoon
and shortly after our return home the boys returned to
school and the gorgeous fall season came as only a Michigan fall can.

Eric was embracing his role as the man of our home.
We have quite a few different pictures from that season
of him and the boys dressed in his favorite team jerseys
standing side by side. We were all experiencing this new
beginning together and the changes seemed so natural and
healthy.

I think that in my mind I had thought that getting remarried would solve all of my problems. I had not prepared myself for the fact that my boys would still spend time at their father's house. Even though we were becoming a family, I would still have to let go at times and they would have to leave. This is a reality of divorce that I was still struggling to make peace with.

I could not shake the emptiness that I felt when the boys were not home with me, and I know it was difficult for Eric to see me go through this. We did not discuss it much, but the pain I endured was affecting him. I would try to prepare myself every time before they left, but it would seem that almost every time the car door would shut, my heart would break. All I wanted to do was numb myself. I could not bring myself to cook or clean or really desire to do anything around the house.

During my brother's time in jail, I hit a new low. We had already lost most of our friends, and the pain from not having my boys with me increased. My brother's friend from New Jersey, Justin, needed a place to stay while he tried to figure out what God was calling him to do next. He had just sold everything to move to Michigan to help with my brother. My husband and I invited him to live in our basement while he was in transition. He felt the pain that my extended family was enduring and became part of our family very naturally. Less than a week after he moved in, Justin helped lead a Bible study for the small group of friends we'd maintained from our old church.

One Saturday afternoon, I was lying on the couch and wallowing in my self-pity when I saw a commercial for a mentoring program in our area. I noted that they needed mentors. I wrote down the number and called them the following Monday. There was a lot of paperwork to fill out, and I talked to a few people about who I was and why I wanted to work with their program. I waited to hear back from them and then I finally received an email that would give me the name of the girl they were going to "match" me with. Even after I was matched, I still would not meet her for a few more weeks. I began to pray for her and our first meeting experience. I prayed for it to be the perfect fit for us both.

In April of 2009, I drove over and was introduced to Rachel for the first time. I promised her that I would not abandon her. I was her fifth mentor since she had started the program. She was only four days older than my oldest son. I was so excited about where this new relationship would lead.

The fall after my brother was released from jail, they packed up their family and moved to North Carolina. The mountains now surrounded them. God knew what He was doing, although the distance has taken a toll on all of us.

A little more than a year into our marriage, at Christmas, Eric and I announced to our family that we had some wonderful news. We were going to have a baby. We told the boys first on Christmas Eve, and they had an understandable mix of different emotions. I was so concerned at how the news would make them feel.

In the second trimester, we learned that I was going to have another boy! The twins would be just shy of eleven when he was born. I enjoyed every second of the pregnancy! I loved how I felt, how I looked, and was filled with such anticipation. The void in my heart was being filled daily and God was healing me through this miracle growing inside of me. The boys were learning how to take care of a pregnant woman with all the accompanying hormones. They were overly concerned about my needs and were sure to not let me carry anything heavy. I remember when I was about seven months along, David told me that he thought that I was looking skinnier—it melted my heart.

I went into labor the night before my thirty-third birthday. Keegan Gibson and I share the same birthday. Another gift from above, I was given another healthy son. We were now a family of six and our new addition was the child that would bring the bond of all of us together through blood.

Within a few weeks of having Keegan, I knew I would not be able to return to work full-time. The desire to stay home only grew stronger during my maternity leave. After much prayer, God gave us the peace to pursue that desire while we trusted Him to provide. We stepped out in faith and I resigned from the wonderful position that God had given to me just a few years before.

The small group Bible study was growing quickly

into a dream to become a church. Our old roommate and new pastor, Justin, got married and now his amazing wife, Anne, accompanied the team as we pursued locations for the church to meet. Tana's husband, Matt, received the job that he bid on so they could move back home. They quickly joined our young church. We relied on God to open up the right doors and He did. We settled on the name of Jericho Road Church. A local bar agreed to let us meet in their facility on Sunday nights because they were closed that day, and they refused our offer to pay rent. We brought a sound system and projector, and set up and tore down each week as God added some new faces to our team little by little. Around this time, we joined the denomination of the Christian and Missionary Alliance. They helped us in our search to find a building of our own. One of our first services held in our new building was our inaugural, candlelight Christmas Eve service in 2009.

Pain Resurfacing

Of them the proverbs are true: "A dog returns to its
vomit," and, "A sow that is washed returns to her
wallowing in the mud."

(2 Peter 2:22)

*The walls have come up and I'm not sure how to
tear them down. I continue to shield my heart
and I don't know how to stop myself from doing
so.*

—journal entry, October 25, 2009

Even though our marriage was beautiful and most of the
time I was happy, I started to realize how scarred I was.
Whenever a disagreement came up, my first reaction was
to push Eric away so I could quickly guard my heart. I
knew that I had developed a very unhealthy pattern for
dealing with hurt, but I didn't know how to change. I
would ask God to help me, and He did, but I still couldn't
stop myself from building up walls when I felt the need to.

Eric had his own way of dealing with the pain he had
experienced in his life. The two of us were committed to
each other and to what God had in store for us, but we
understood that we were going to need help to get us there

too. We found Doyle, a man of God who was a pastor and also pursuing his counseling degree. We asked him to meet with us. Every time we went to see him, we learned more about the art of communication in a relationship. As we met with him, we grew. Sometimes it didn't seem like it, but we continued to meet with him.

There isn't a neat three-step program for dealing with past hurts or successfully building a blended family. It is much harder than it would seem, and this process of healing was going to take a lot of work to get through the difficult stages that would come our way.

I wanted what every girl wants. I wanted Eric to love me. I wanted him to love my children. I wanted the happily-ever-after dream that all the other girls seemed to have. When I wasn't getting my way, I would pout and complain. I would push him away and think negative thoughts about our marriage. I would let those thoughts control my mood until I was ready to be happy again and then I would expect him to bounce back to that place when I was ready. For some reason, that wasn't how he processed things (imagine that!). If we were going to move forward and reach the potential that God had for us, I knew I was going to have to change. I wanted that change, but I felt stuck. I knew that changing my behavior was going to require me to go back to my past and begin unraveling the different lies that the enemy had brought to my heart and mind over time. It was going to take a lot of work.

One night, Eric and I were out on a date when I began

having a flashback to a season of pain from my past. The fear that I lived with over whether or not he would leave me consumed my life on a regular basis. We were at a small concert and the song and artists singing brought back memories from my past. I got up to go to the bathroom and I couldn't bring myself to return to the auditorium where the concert was being held. I was literally paralyzed with fear. Eric had no idea what was going on. He was inside enjoying the concert and I had to go get in our car because of what was going on in my heart.

After the concert let out, he came to the car and I tried to explain to him what my heart was feeling during our drive home, but it was hard for him to understand fully. I knew that my thoughts were ridiculous. I didn't expect myself to act that way. I had been looking forward to spending time with him while my parents watched Keegan for us. I sensed that he felt overwhelmed with my needs and we both knew that I was going to need to meet with our counselor again to work through these thoughts and fears.

This was the first time that I allowed myself to go back and deal with the memories that I had tucked away for years. I didn't want them to surface now. I didn't understand why they were, but I knew that I had to deal with them and face them head-on in order for me to find deliverance from these memories.

I couldn't continue to project my fears and insecurities onto Eric. I needed to own them for myself and recognize that my level of expectation was too high, largely because of my past wounds. As I began to dig into my thoughts, I started to realize that I believed things about Eric that were not even real, and I knew that the enemy was using my past to put these thoughts into my mind.

I had to let the Lord change my thoughts and begin facing these lies with the strength that was somewhere deep down inside of me. I knew the truths that I wanted to believe, and I could hold on to them on my good days. But the bad days would still dictate my life forever unless I allowed the change to finally come.

And so I began to ask God to heal me fully, whatever it would take.

My Calling Begins

When you pass through the waters, I will be with you; and when you pass through the rivers, they will not sweep over you. When you walk through the fire, you will not be burned; the flames will not set you ablaze.

(Isaiah 43:2)

Feeling You move in small ways. I'm thankful for it though. The road ahead will be painful. I will continue to lean on you, Lord, for wisdom with each new day.

—journal entry, February 16, 2011

I began to go back and read my old journals to help me deal with my emotions and to discover what I needed to remember. Through this process, God continued to speak to my heart. I felt Him calling me toward Himself. I listened intently and tried to discover more of my purpose through everything I was feeling. I kept asking Him to stretch me and to renew me, and He kept listening. God woke me up early one morning and led me to write a letter asking for forgiveness from many different people in our community. I had been holding each of them captive through bitter-

ness and the letter allowed a beautiful feeling of release
to sweep through me. I got this idea from a book that our
pastor wrote called *Love Mission*. One of the missions in
the book is to write a letter to someone you need to forgive,
and that morning I sat down and wrote out seven letters.

After staying home with Keegan for six months, our fi-
nances were being heavily stretched, and I decided to start
working again. I sent my resume out to the city of North
Muskegon. They posted a part-time position that seemed
like a great match for our needs. The Lord gave me the job
and it was even more perfect then we had first thought.
The pay and hours lined up to be exactly what I had been
praying for. We also learned of a nanny looking for work,
and we asked her if she'd be interested in a part-time job. I
remember driving to work every day and being so thankful
for this new opportunity.

That February, my husband went on a missions trip
to Thailand, and I was looking forward to some alone
time with the Lord while he was gone. I had forgotten
how good it felt to just sit at the feet of Jesus and talk with
him, instead of tuning out by watching TV. His presence
was incredible. A good friend named Alli came over one
night, and we spent the evening together in prayer. She has
inspired me greatly by her understanding of His power and
by her desire to encourage others. As God was moving and
answering my prayers, I was not exactly sure how to handle
everything that He was throwing my way. I began to do a
study on Satan, and I decided to camp out and meditate

on Job's story. I was so intrigued that at the beginning of the book of Job, we learn that Satan was able to enter God's presence, and, even stranger, that God pointed Job out to Satan as someone he should consider to devour.

> "One day the angels came to present themselves before the LORD, and Satan also came with them. The LORD said to Satan, 'Where have you come from?' Satan answered the LORD, 'From roaming throughout the earth, going back and forth on it.' Then the LORD said to Satan, 'Have you considered my servant Job? There is no one on earth like him; he is blameless and upright, a man who fears God and shuns evil.'"
>
> (Job 1: 6–8)

After reading these verses, I envisioned God believing in me as much as He did in Job, and that inspired me even more to become all that He knew I could be.

Being newlyweds, Eric and I were slowly learning how to become one. God was doing such a work in our hearts to help us with this. He was stretching and molding us into the image that He had intended for us. In marriage, we are always working toward becoming one. I have loved this journey with my beloved husband. His firm foundation in Christ has inspired me to be the wife that I have always wanted to be.

While God was working in my heart and calling me to be set free from past wounds, I was introduced to a woman named Sophia. I had been praying that God would bring people into my life who could speak to me with wisdom. She was staying at my parent's guest home when I met her.

She had come to be alone with the Lord and to focus on the ministry that she leads.

Years before, Sophia felt God call her to start a ministry for migrant children. She desired to tell these dear little ones about God's love for them as well as to teach them more English. I was so inspired by her humility and obedience to the calling over her life. After we shared our hearts with one another, she encouraged me to fast and pray with her for God to show us His will regarding my hurts. Even though I had a complicated history with food and eating, I do believe in the power of fasting and its significance in preparing our hearts to receive what God had for us. The second day into our fast, Sophia gave me seven handwritten pages filled with scripture for me to refer to when I was praying. I began using those pages to pray, and I still refer to them frequently. I know that they came from Him for me.

It was almost like God unleashed a whole new concept to me with those pages from Sophia. I remember looking over the verses and "praying scripture" for the first time. It was amazing. God opened my eyes to understanding more of the power that we have in His word. God has continued to show me the significance we have in going to His word to find the answers to questions that we may be wrestling with.

Sometimes, when I am overcome with a certain feeling that the enemy wants to lie to me about in my life, I will find verses that help me pray through that emotion. I'll go to the internet and search for something like: verses on trusting, calling, hope, pain, waiting, or pride. I click on the first link and there I find twenty-five verses to read about that topic. Usually I'll skim through them until I land on the one that speaks to my spirit the most, and then I will write it down on a sticky note and put it in a place where I know I will continue to see it for the rest of the day. I also like to have at least one verse in my van for when I am driving and need to have Him calm my restless spirit.

Two months after I first met Sophia, I drove out to see her on the night before her team would begin their day camp for that summer. When I arrived there, I was awed by the natural beauty of this place the Lord had brought her to accomplish His vision.

In 2006, she started the first day camp after spending a few years building relationships with some students in the local schools by teaching them English. In 2011, her team hosted over two hundred children for their summer program where they shared Jesus with them all. I asked Sophia when she became aware that God had called her to this ministry, and she said that she thinks it was always with her. She does not remember this passion ever not being part of her life. I shared with her my burden for ministering to women and how I did not know where to start. She paused and said in her sweet, quiet country voice, "Maybe you have already started on your path, but you're just now realizing it." I have thought about that idea more, and now I believe that was exactly the truth I needed to hear.

I took Rachel, the young girl that I mentor, with me that on that trip. She and I were able to pray with Sophia and her team the night we were there. It was a wonderful trip for both of us, and I am so thankful for that night of memories we share.

Knowing Your Calling

. . . for God's gifts and his call are irrevocable.
(Romans 11:29)

*Father God—I'm pretty overwhelmed by your
presence in my life right now. You knew this was
where my heart would go during this season.
Who am I to ever question the path that I have
to walk? I wish that I could pause this moment
in time with you tonight.*
—*journal entry, May 18, 2011*

What holds you back from fullybelieving in yourself? I
think we all have a specific dream somewhere deep within
us. Why is it that so many of us give up on believing that
God could also want that dream for us? I know so many
creative people who can do anything. I used to struggle
with jealousy of these people. I'm the kind of girl who has
tried to find her creative hand in almost everything. I've
tried knitting, scrap-booking, cooking, decorating, craft-
ing, sewing, singing, and playing the guitar. The list could
really go on and on if I cared to share. And while I like to

do some of those things, I get bored doing them. I simply do not have the passion required to pursue any of these activities.

I have always had a passion for writing, and I get excited when I get to listen to someone tell me their story. I cannot describe how alive I feel now when I think about the idea of telling other women about who God is and what He is doing in my heart. It is my passion and I know it is my calling. It continues to fuel me when I have a heavy heart.

Someone told me recently that if you look back on your life and the experiences you have gathered, you could almost get a glimpse of where God is taking you. When I heard this, it renewed my excitement to read back through my old journals and blog posts from the last few years.

One night after I began to go back and read from my past, Eric and I had a short conversation in the car. I said to him that I thought I should write a book, and his response changed my life. He said "I think you should, honey." I wasn't expecting that response from him. In fact, I was only joking when I said it. The fact that he agreed with me caught me off guard and made me think more about it. He drove us to Barnes & Noble and told me to find a book on how to write a book. As I walked off in search of guide-books, my confidence began to build. I came home and started writing that very night. The determination to write and publish a book became a driving force in my life.

While reading through my old journals, I actually

grew scared as I thought about what God could possibly want for me in this process of becoming. My journal revealed God-sized dreams for my life and the future, and the unknown was so intimidating.

I told my husband about my fear, and how I wished I did not feel this way. I wished that I could simply go about my normal life like I once had. I did not understand why I had taken the risk to discover more of what He created me to be. It all seemed too big and out of my control, but I knew I couldn't turn back. Something told me to continue to move forward. I asked God to slow me down, to give me a direction for each new decision I needed to make, whether simple decisions or complex. I began to learn to find rest even when it didn't make sense to me.

I have learned that there is safety to be found in trusting God. Eric and I hit a crossroads with my job situation again. God planted the idea for me to write this book, so I obeyed and began writing. In the very same week, our nanny told us that she had taken a new job somewhere else and couldn't keep working for us. Although I was very excited about writing, I was not ready to quit my job and pursue writing full-time. I needed to hear from the Lord. I wanted to be sure that I had others praying with me too. I was discovering that while I wrote, my heart was also being inspired to reach out and begin speaking to women about my journey.

I had just completed a study on the book of Esther in the Old Testament, and I was inspired by her life. Like

Esther, I called on some of my closest friends to join me in prayer and fasting for the next three days. I had sensed that God was trying to speak to me, and I asked them to join me in seeking Him to receive what that was.

On the second day of the fast, I found myself asking the Lord to show me what I was supposed to do. I needed some kind of sign, something, really anything. I was willing to stay put at my job, but I was willing to take a new step of faith too. I knew that caring well for our four sons, working, writing, and keeping up with the home would be difficult, but I didn't want to act on something before the Lord gave me the peace to move forward in this direction. On my way home from work the next day, I was in this conversation with the Lord asking Him once again to reveal to me what it was that He wanted me to do with this new passion growing in my spirit. As I drove past an exit, I saw a sign with the word BIG on it, and something in my spirit grabbed onto that word. I didn't hear an audible voice; I just knew that the word was for me and that it was from Him. I started crying tears of joy in the van. Why God? Why? I'm not worthy for you to use me, I said. I was filled with such a joy. I know that He visited me in my vehicle, and I praised Him the rest of the way home.

Eric and I carefully rearranged our budget, and the following Monday I resigned from my job.

I have always had a passion to encourage women, but God had given me a whole new kind of burden to do so during this season of my life. Where in the world would I start articulating what God was showing me to do? I'm sure I sounded like a crazy woman to anyone I talked to while I was in this transition. I struggled to clearly express this passion in my heart for a while. My Spirit had been ignited in a way that I know came from God, and He was telling me that things were not going to be the same anymore. I didn't know how to express the confidence that lay beneath that. I just knew that once again I was going to need to trust the Lord to lead me on this new journey. And that's what I did. I put my heart out there for Him to hold and I learned that He is safe and loving, and because of that, it just felt . . . right.

In the past, I had moved ahead of God when I got an idea in my head. With this new passion of mine, I had to be sure to let the Lord God Almighty be in complete control. I knew that it would be my human nature to move quickly through some of the processes, and I had to hold my tongue and remind myself to slow down. I had to learn to be still and wait for God's timing with everything. I know that I still have a lot to learn about patience, but I do see slow growth in this area of my life.

> *"I have had such restlessness in my heart*
> *and soul for the last few weeks while trying*
> *to hear from you, Lord, and now I'm just*
> *going to sit back and let you show me. I*
> *would screw this up for sure."*
> —journal entry, August 6, 2011

". . . but those who hope in the LORD will renew their strength. They will soar on wings like eagles; they will run and not grow weary, they will walk and not be faint."

(Isaiah 40:31)

When I read this verse and other verses on the subject of waiting, I am able to see that there is a healthy way of anticipating and letting God lead us on the path He wants us to travel. In Galatians chapter five, we learn about the fruits of the Spirit, and I'm intrigued that these characteristics are described as a food. As we grow in our understanding of who God is, and He reveals more of Himself to us, our spirits actually begin to grow and take on His characteristics. When we are lacking in one of the fruits that His Spirit offers us, we can search the scriptures to discover "food" that will help us grow in that area. God gives this to us as He begins to reveal more of Himself to us through His Spirit living inside of us.

I have been asking God to develop in me the fruit of patience. I know that I need growth in this area of my life and only He can bring traits into my life that will be the best for me and for my future. Because I cannot see what lies ahead, I trust that the Creator of the Universe already knows every detail of it and has already been there with me through those experiences. I would much rather let Him be the one guiding my path because of this.

He replied, 'Because you have so little faith. Truly I tell you, if you have faith as small as a mustard seed, you can say to this mountain, 'Move from here to there,' and it will move. Nothing will be impossible for you.

(Matthew 17:20)

This passage came up in one of my studies, and I have tried to grasp the significance of a tiny mustard seed and see why it was that Jesus compared it with faith. I have been asking God to give me this mustard seed faith for my future, and I've found so many different things while digging into it. Each insight pointed toward a deeper understanding of my potential growth. Every seed that has been planted will eventually need watering for survival. These seeds will also need sunlight, and they will need time for the desired growth to take place. And then, when the season is right, the bountiful and beautiful harvest will come.

This lesson of waiting has definitely been the hardest to learn. I suspect it probably is for many others too. I have gotten in front of God so many times in my life and then He has had to lovingly pull me back and redirect me. There have been times when He tried to do this gently and I wouldn't listen. Sometimes He has had to put freight trains in my path to get my attention.

One day I was driving in our minivan with all four of our boys. We were on our way to visit my parents for the afternoon, and we were just a few miles away from their house when a train stopped us. As we waited we discussed how this train being in front of us had a purpose, and we came up with a few possibilities. Just as it was about to clear the crossing, the train came to a complete stop. We continued to wait patiently. A few minutes passed by and then I made the executive decision to turn our minivan around and escape this obstacle by taking a different route. As we drove away, the boys began to bet whether or not they thought the train would be gone by the time we got to the road that led to my parent's house from the other side. When we came around the corner from the new direction, there was no trace of the train. My oldest said, "Why do you think that happened, Mom?" I said I thought it was another lesson in patience that God was trying to teach me. If I had waited just a minute longer, I would have been able to cross without going out of my way.

The Attack

Then you will know the truth, and the truth will set you free.

(John 8:32)

So much has happened over the last few months. It's been a very tough journey. I've had to learn to peel off layers of pain from my past and I've felt attacked so intensely doing so. The Lord has been so faithful. He is my foundation and constant redeemer.

—journal entry, July 16, 2011

God's truth is the key that can unlock the doors we have sealed shut and vowed never to reopen again. As I mentioned before, I had struggled for years with being a closet smoker. I made commitments to myself a million times to quit this consuming activity.

Years ago, I stopped over for a visit with my parents one day and I had a very powerful conversation about my smoking with my father. He said something that inspired me. "Jennifer, you have been told a lie from the devil about these cigarettes." I asked what the lie was, and he said, "The lie is what you need to figure out for yourself." I went home and wrote down some of the lies I thought I'd been told, and they began to lose their power over me from that day forward. The truth was, I couldn't afford the cigarettes, they were killing me, it did stink, my kids would find out someday, one more cigarette would continue to lead to another, it was affecting my relationship with God, and I didn't like how they made me feel. As the lies began to slip away, I knew I could quit.

What if we realized that God wants to use us just where we are? What if we understood that Jesus knows our deepest sin and still loves us. I love the story told in John chapter 4 about the woman at the well. The passage says that Jesus had to go through Samaria. He came upon a well where He would be in line to get some water. He had a purpose for going to the well and it was for her. He knew that this special woman would be there and He knew her future in Him. She was a woman who had been with five men already and was now onto living with the next. He told her who He was. He believed in her even in spite of her past mistakes and He wanted to use her to change her city. All it would take was for her to believe in Him and to believe that what He had to offer her could change her life if she would let it. He knows each of our stories too and He wants to use them for His Glory.

"I can't seem to shake this feeling tonight.
I am feeling like I have this dream within
reach and that it might all get snatched

*away. I am trying ever so dearly to keep
moving forward and to stay encouraged
about what I feel like God has been calling
me to. I feel so weak. I am being pressed
with the thoughts of unworthiness and that
the mountain is too high for my climbing.
I have never been too consistent in my
emotions. I have been known to be an all
or nothing girl. That can be good when
I'm in the all mode, but has proven to be incredibly damaging when the nothing
mode kicks in. I wish that there was more
of an in-between. I know I need to strive for
that and so tonight that will be my prayer.
Help me, Lord, to be more consistent
when the waves start to stir. I long to be
more like you. Show me what lessons I need
to learn on this journey into becoming who
you created me to be."*
—journal entry, August 1, 2011

My husband and I decided that we should take a sabbati-
cal from our roles in the church during the spring before
I started writing my book. Eric was the worship director
and I had worked with the children and women's ministry
there.

We were both plowing through our weeks, full steam
ahead with rarely any breaks. We knew we couldn't keep

this pace up, and we needed a break if we wanted to continue to serve our church well. We decided to spend a season strengthening our family. We were still newlyweds and both working jobs outside of our church too. Every week, we struggled just to make it to church, in part due to increasing pressures at home that led us to dig into our past hurts and find freedom. After a few months of focused counseling and with a renewed vigor, we agreed that it was a good time for us to return to our roles at the church.

The Saturday before my husband would return to leading worship, I woke up feeling an overwhelming sense of evil. I spent some time reading the Bible and praying that the feeling would go away, but it did not. It actually increased as the day went on and I could not shake it.

I had this little voice in my head telling me that I would never finish my book. And worse than that, the voice mocked the idea that anybody would ever listen to me and find value in me speaking to other women. I nearly deleted everything that I had written in a fit of rage. I allowed this attitude of defeat into our home that afternoon. Looking back, I see an attack of spiritual oppression at its finest. There is really no other explanation in my mind for where those thoughts came from.

The next morning, I woke up and looked over at my husband and said, "We made it." We prayed twice together before he left for the church. I cannot tell you how incredibly proud I was to be married to the man leading worship on that stage that morning. He came alive as he led the songs. He was doing what he was created to do by leading us all in corporate worship. What a wonderful and memorable day for our family.

The enemy knew how important that day was going to be for so many. After the preaching, there would be a baptism. We were so privileged to watch our neighbors go forward and proudly claim their new life in Christ. After we got back home, our neighbor Cory sent my husband a message letting him know that he was a big reason why Cory chose to be baptized.

When we start living openly and turning the light on our secrets, something starts to happen in heavenly places. The enemy does not want us to be set free from the oppression of darkness. It's not for no reason that he is called a thief and a liar. I am so excited to see what lies ahead for our ministry as we continue to try to live transparently for the congregation to see.

My Dream

Therefore, I urge you, brothers and sisters, in view of God's mercy, to offer your bodies as a living sacrifice, holy and pleasing to God—this is your true and proper worship. Do not conform to the pattern of this world, but be transformed by the renewing of your mind. Then you will be able to test and approve what God's will is—His good, pleasing and perfect will.

(Romans 12:1–2)

Today Tana and I had a photo shoot and a meeting at the Shoreline Inn for our conference next fall. Wow—I sure can't believe that we are on this journey.

—journal entry, September 14, 2011

I had a phone conversation recently with a woman I had never met in person. She and I spent an hour over the phone praying together. She would ask a question and then pause to listen to my answer. It was the first of many conversations I would have with different people that God placed in my life to encourage me to revisit my past hurts. The end of our conversation will stick with me forever. She had me read a verse and then we finished our conversation in prayer.

> The weapons we fight with are not the weapons of the
> world. On the contrary, they have divine power to de-
> molish strongholds. We demolish arguments and every
> pretension that sets itself up against the knowledge of
> God, and we take captive every thought to make it obe-
> dient to Christ. And we will be ready to punish every
> act of disobedience, once your obedience is complete.
>
> (2 Corinthians 10:4–6)

I am still trying to fully understand this passage, and God keeps drawing me back to these same verses again and again. I love how God does this. He is always trying to show Himself to us. He speaks to us in so many different ways.

We all battle the lies that plague our minds every day. We begin to believe these lies, and they eventually knock us off our path to discover the truth about our purpose. I know that the Lord is calling me to trust Him to lead and to understand the depth of His great love for me. This love has always been with me, even when I was hurting the most. I refuse to let the enemy pull me back from this path that I am traveling.

One of the ways that you can protect yourself on your journey is by surrounding yourself with the strong friends that God places in your life. Together they can help you to chase after the dreams that He has placed in your heart. The more people that you talk to about your God-given desires, the more accountable you become.

I am amazed by the incredible women that God has

placed in my life, to encourage and partner with me for all that God has in store. When you have friends that are living in obedience to God's will for their lives, you feel so powerful. We become mighty warriors and we are able to reach new territory through our potential in Him.

God answered a prayer of mine many years ago when I asked for a Christian friend to come and encourage me in life. Over ten years now, Tana and I have shared a special friendship that many women never find. I am so incredibly grateful for this woman that the Lord brought to me when I cried out to Him. God continues to write our stories and is allowing our paths to walk close to one another for now and, I know, for years to come.

When I felt God's stirring in my heart, I met up with her for coffee and I began to share with her what God was doing. We talked for a few hours and then we began to dream together of what God could do with our testimonies. She began to catch a glimpse of my dream. The next week, she would be one of many women fasting and praying with me to hear from the Lord about my future. One of the first ideas we landed on together was the vision of a conference for women.

> Take delight in the LORD, and he will give you the desires of your heart.
>
> (Psalms 37:4)

I keep asking Him the question, what does it mean to delight myself in You, Lord?

One night my husband and I were lying in bed talking and I asked him to tell me his largest dream. I asked, "If there was just one hope in the deepest part of your heart, the biggest thing your imagination could dream, what would that be?" He knew his answer right away, but then took a moment to put it into words that conveyed the extent of his longing. His dream was that one day he would lead thousands of people in worship. With joy I told him that I believe that is who God created him to be. I know the things that He has been putting in my heart lately to think about and dream about, and I believe that as I continue to discover how to take great pleasure in Him these desires will become something attainable.

I've been asking God for wisdom on how to begin walking in the direction of my calling and true purpose in Him. I feel like He has been gently guiding me there.

I started writing a daily verse on a small dry-erase board on our fridge. Here is one of our favorites:

> If you, then, though you are evil, know how to give good gifts to your children, how much more will your Father in heaven give good gifts to those who ask him!
>
> (Matthew 7:11)

I think of all the things I've wanted or thought I needed, but that I never really took the time to ask Him to provide for first. I have asked for some things and not gotten them, but usually I simply forget to ask for the basics.

Recently I wrote out a small list of things that our

family would need in the next few months—school clothes, a briefcase, dresser, couch for sitting room, etc. These are things that I would have just purchased in the past, without even asking Him to provide for us first. I simply never made it a priority to ask Him for things, unless it was out of desperation. Wow . . . that's so sad. I have been so amazed to watch how God works to provide for us when we ask Him to. In fact, one of the things on my list was something we never found the time or money for—a family vacation. I am typing this while I sit in the dining room of a lovely Connecticut home right now on our family vacation to the East Coast.

> *"Forgive me, Lord. I don't want to only need*
> *you when things are desperate. I want to*
> *need you throughout every day for every*
> *little detail of my life. I can't make it one*
> *day without you holding my hand. That's*
> *how close I want us to be. Thank you, daddy,*
> *for giving me such peace today."*
> —journal entry September 15, 2011

God first birthed a vision in my mind to speak to women, and I have decided to move forward in following this call. I have had such an igniting in my spirit to write this book and to begin a ministry in my community for women who are experiencing the same kind of hurt I lived through.

Since starting this adventure, I have had confirmation after confirmation that this is the direction the Lord wants me to take. But I also question and wonder about His power and the direction this road will lead, just as the children of Israel were able to follow God's signs and also carry great fear and doubt while searching for the Promised Land.

> By day the LORD went ahead of them in a pillar of cloud to guide them on their way and by night in a pillar of fire to give them light, so that they could travel by day or night.
>
> (Exodus 13:21)

I can't tell you how many times I have looked toward the heavens while driving to look for "my cloud." I am always asking God to show Himself to me when I am in nature or in a place where I feel His presence. Some wouldn't believe it when I say this, but nearly every time I ask God to show Himself to me in the clouds, He does. I usually just see His eyes. Maybe it is only in my mind, but I allow myself to believe that the two blue circles forming between the white clouds appear to me just because I ask. One time, I saw a giant cloud shaped like a heart. I didn't notice it until I was in the middle of praying in my car, and then I asked Him to show Himself. I know He put it there just for me.

After I had left my job, I made it my top priority to begin meeting with as many women in our community as I could. I wanted to hear their stories, and I wanted to share with them what God was doing in my heart. I filled up my calendar every week. I started inviting them over to my home during Keegan's nap schedule, and I made a lot of new friends. God continued to lead new faces and unusual situations my way. He used each of them to help me to understand Him more. I began to realize that I had placed Him inside a box long ago, and now I was open to Him showing me Himself in any way that He wanted to. And He was.

During this time, Tana and I continued to grow and dream. The idea to host a conference seemed like an easy thing to do, but where in the world should we start? We scheduled a meeting at a nice hotel here in town that had a conference space. We got dressed up for the afternoon as we met and toured with the hotel's conference coordinator. I remember feeling professional and prepared for the questions that would come my way about what the "conference" would look like. Truthfully, all we had was a name. We had no money.

As we waited for the coordinator to come into the room, I thought back on my corporate job from a few years before and the many meetings that had been held in our conference room. Although I didn't attend many of those meetings, I know that being comfortable in a business environment gave me the peace that I needed for the meeting that we would soon have. I had a strong confidence in who I was and also in the dream that had been placed in my heart.

We met with two women to discuss our dream for a big event that we were planning for a year out. The space they had available seemed too small for the dream in our hearts, and as we flipped through their folder with information, our hearts began to envision what was becoming for the future of the "Legacy Conference."

As Tana and I drove away from that first meeting, we had to chuckle. We were driving away in my minivan, two "professional" conference planners headed home to take care of our children.

The women at Jericho Road were catching our vision too and joining our dream without hesitation. A few weeks later, I went to a different hotel with a team member to view the layout of their conference center. A local business group was using the conference room, hallway, and breakout rooms for their event, and we could picture our conference being held there so easily. This hotel was also twice as big, and they were eager for our business. We continued to dream big.

We soon settled on the Holiday Inn as our location, and the name "Legacy," with the tag line "Seasons of Beauty." But we still had no money. Although we were asking God to bring us the breakout speakers, we still had not secured a venue. One by one the team was forming and members were coming from all over. The connections were coming together from God Himself. It was awesome to hear each woman that joined the team share with us how God had showed them that they were supposed to be joining us.

During this season, I had transitioned at my church from the children's ministry over to the women's ministry. Our pastor's wife, Anne, and I were team-teaching a series on the fruits of the Spirit. As I drove to our very first study, I prayed for God's favor.

Just before the study started that morning, Anne told me that an anonymous gift had come in for the conference. She handed me $1,000 in cash. I literally got on my knees in front of all the women there to say a prayer of thanks to the Lord. We had not shared with many our need for any money. The deposit amount needed to secure the hotel was half of this amount. To know that God impressed on someone's heart to give toward this event meant so much to me.

We ordered business cards, scheduled a day to sign a contract with the Holiday Inn for the event, and opened up our bank account. Our church agreed to help us open an account for Legacy so we could begin taking in gifts and paying for expenses. The morning that I would put down our deposit and sign our contract with the hotel, I realized while I was journaling that I was going to the hotel exactly one year before the event that we'd be hosting. That was more than a coincidence.

We held our first team meeting a few weeks later, and over forty ladies attended to hear about our vision for the community.

I am uncertain of how many Legacy conferences we will host. In fact, we may only do one. The Lord continues

to lead, and I do my best to follow. I hope and pray that the
Lord will open up the doors and allow for opportunities
to continue coming our way, but I don't know the future—
only God does. For now, I just know that I am on the path
that He wants for me to be on and that I can trust Him
with the road ahead.

To the Ends of the Earth

But you will receive power when the Holy Spirit comes on you; and you will be my witnesses in Jerusalem, and in all Judea and Samaria, and to the ends of the earth.

(Acts 1:8)

I received my first edit back from the editor yesterday. I am praying that the Lord will help me to work on my next stage to have the words that He wants for me to have with this project. I am so excited and hopeful.

—journal entry, March 1, 2012

When I began to talk to other women about the dream that Tana and I had of hosting a women's conference, I saw the excitement captivate hearts quickly. As I write tonight, we are still seven months away from our first conference and my excitement continues to burn with intensity as we get closer to it. It is almost as though the Lord has given my spirit a glimpse of what's to come with this conference ministry and its future. I don't feel pressured to have to do all the right things. I have recognized from day one that this was something that He put in my heart to do and my being obedient to the promptings was the first step. I continue to learn the dance of letting Him lead the way and I just pray that I grow in the understanding of how to follow well.

We are incredibly blessed to live on the property and in the house that my husband grew up in. Our ranch style home has been in the family for a few generations now. On the property of over twenty acres sits more than a dozen large greenhouses. My father-in-law owns and runs them still today. This past winter, I discovered that they would be a wonderful place for me to walk since they could provide me with shelter from the wind and snow whenever I got time to sneak away from the family for some quiet time and exercise. I have so enjoyed my prayer time in these greenhouses. I have watched seeds sown and baskets fill over the last few months. While I am in there, I ask God to take me all around the world to share my story and His love with others. I am willing to go, if He will send me. I long to touch lives for His Glory. I refuse to limit what He wants to do with my life. I will never put Him in a box again. He's so BIG!

I have found a new love in writing and I have already starting writing a second book. I know that God will continue to grow this passion of mine and I am so excited to see that transform over the years.

My brother, Jerry, and his wife, Jamie, did find healing while living in the mountains. They quickly found a community to reach out to and began to minister again. They had been struck down, but were not destroyed.

I am happy to say that we have a good relationship with my former husband and that God has brought much healing to broken places from the past. Kyle has continued to provide support and has been a consistent role in our boys lives for which I am very thankful. I serve a God who can make beauty out of ashes, all in His time.

Before this past year I don't think I ever really believed that God would or could use me for anything great. I had made so many poor choices in my life and I kept finding myself feeling as though I wasn't worthy of living a life of abundance, stability, happiness, or success. I thought that only the people who made all the right choices were able to receive such blessings. I realize now that those "perfect" people don't really exist.

When I began to write out my story, I saw that I had a powerful one to share. Part of the power behind it lay deep within my past mistakes, the very things that held me back from sharing all along. I had bought into the lie that told me that I was alone in making these choices and that others could not relate to me or be able to be inspired or taught by me because of them. I am so thankful that the Lord led me to truth.

As women, we carry heavy loads. We fill so many different roles in our lives, and it is very easy for us to never find the time to discover our true purpose or calling. Our lives fill up with busyness, and we wonder why we are so unfulfilled and left longing for more. Some of us are overwhelmed with the responsibilities in our homes and still carry full-time jobs outside of them. I can promise you that if you are not carving out time to be alone with the Lord each day, you will eventually hit a point of feeling like giving up.

I challenge you to make a new commitment to get up early to spend some time alone with the Lord before you start your day. Do it tomorrow. I understand that some of you may have unique schedules and that another time during the day might work better for you. The point is, start somewhere. I want you to feel fulfilled and full of His power and love. He wants to show you His plans and desires for your life. He longs to have a relationship with you. I don't care what your past is. God has already forgiven and set you free from that past. I promise you that He can use every situation you have been through for His glory if you will let Him.

I also want to encourage you to begin to journal if you don't keep one already. It is a wonderful way to share your heart with others down the road. It also allows you to look back at the things God has done for you. When I think about my life, one of the things that I am most inspired by is the legacy that I hope to leave behind for my children.

Ladies, do you know how important your role in the home is? Proverbs 14:1 says "The wise woman builds her house, but with her own hands the foolish one tears hers down."

If we are going to reach the ones that we love, then we

have to start understanding our roles more clearly. It will always start within our homes first. We must love our husbands and our children with the love the Lord has shown us. And as we are faithful to this role, the Lord can and will give us more opportunities to show others the love that He has given us.

Maybe you aren't ready to talk about your own story yet. Maybe you are just able to listen to someone else's story right now. But let me urge you to start somewhere. Begin keeping a journal, or find a close friend who will let you start to share your own dreams and fears. If you continue living in fear, as I did for so long, things will never change in your life. In order for us to make a mark in this world and share God's love with others, we all have to take the first step.

There is nothing special about me. The Lord wants to use you and He will if you let Him. If you begin to trust and share your heart and passions with Him and others, You will begin to discover your purpose and His calling for your life.

About the Author

Jennifer Wagenmaker is the visionary founder of Legacy Ministries. She shares her story boldly and transparently with women all over the world. Raised in a pastor's home, Jennifer learned of the Savior's love for her at a young age, and she is filled with a great passion to share this love with others. She'll inspire you to dream God-sized dreams for your life.

Jennifer lives with her husband, Eric, and their four sons in West Michigan.

Interior design by Eric Wagenmaker Design
Typeset in Minion Pro 11/15.6
by Eric Wagenmaker
Printed on acid-free paper

CPSIA information can be obtained at www.ICGtesting.com
Printed in the USA
BVOW040100060313

314804BV00002B/6/P